I0469800

Vimal Vachhani

The Mindful Manager

A guide to getting things done and finding
purpose in what you do

betterment.studio

Download the free Companion App!

Android

IOS

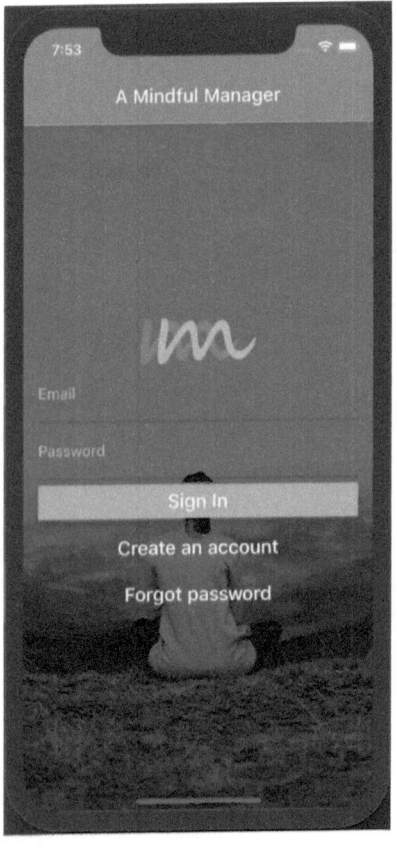

My Other Books

1) Jack of All Trades Master of Some; An Introduction to Consulting
2) An Introduction to Consulting - A Primer: An abridged and essentials guide from the book: Jack of All Trades Master of Some, an Introduction to Consulting
3) The Solar System; A STEM book for children

Who is This Book for?

This book is not just for managers, workers or mindfulness and flow practitioners. This book has been written for anyone looking to get more done in less time and get more value out of their work. The lessons and tips in this book are for anyone wanting to find a greater balance in what they do and live in a happier state while doing so. We all want to live a life with less stress and anxiety. Both of which are leading factors in depression that, in turn, can lead to a lack of purpose and meaning in one's life. If we are more deliberate with how we spend our time and sharpen our ability to focus, we can become creators of great works that we can be proud of. If you are a young new hire looking to move up in the workforce, or an entrepreneur looking to build a business, this book is for you. If you are an artist looking to create or a DIY'er looking to build something in your spare time, this book is for you. If you want to spend more time with your family and less time at work, this book is also for you. The lessons shared in this book can be applied to all parts of your life. Being an organized minimalist while being strategic with your time will obtain you velocity gains in your daily activities and help you move the needle on your whole life.

Introduction

Work. Most of us must go to it or complete it in some form or fashion every day. Professional work takes up a third of our days from Monday to Friday, while our personal lives cut into the second slice of that pie. This leaves just a few hours for downtime and pleasurable activities before we spend the last third of our day sleeping.

Around two years prior to when I began writing this book, I had hit a personal wall in my life. I found myself unhappy with my work and, more importantly, my work-life balance. I was working harder and longer than I ever had in the past, but I felt as if I was accomplishing less and creating work of less significance. Outside of work, I was the type to have multiple side projects at all times, but I even found less time and passion for those. The lack of creativity outside of work led to more frustrations that bled into my professional work, thus creating a vicious cycle of displeasure and lowered production of output.

I found others that shared my misery and I narrowed it down to two primary types of personalities that usually complained they were unhappy or frustrated with their present life. There were those who dwelled in the past and there were those who always daydreamed about the future – both never realizing that "the present" they were not content with was actually the place they never quite lived in. I'd always been a forward thinker. I used to be told I was a daydreamer, but over time, the line between daydreaming and stressfully living out future scenarios that may never occur blurred without me even realizing it. However, this time was different. I started to dwell on the past. I recalled times early on in my career or even in college where I could go heads down for long stretches of time, diligently working on one task to completion. I was stubbornly focused and losing hours and sunlight without realizing it was happening. It was this mode of work I could shift into so easily that I personally accredited to my success in school and the workforce. Now, I sat angry and frustrated that the skill had deteriorated and I could not figure out when or how it happened. Unbeknownst to me, I had taken a big step forward in my personal development. I realized that I had a problem, but the part that eluded me was how to go about solving the issue. So, I did what most people do, I began googling my problems. I read through hundreds of articles on flow and productivity, I read books on happiness and millionaire success habits by life coaches. I downloaded a meditation application and began attending meditation classes at a Buddhist temple close to my home. I self-experimented with my findings. Some I found were difficult changes to make, others were simple. Some I found worked and some did not provide the lift I was hoping for. Some changes were logical and practical while others were off the wall, but I tried as many as I could. Maybe in a future book, I will explain the reasoning and result of finding a large tree in a park and giving it a hug.

After two years, I've hit a great personal stride, but I am very much in the infancy of my journey. Even with the small steps taken, I have found huge successes. In the last year, in addition to having a successful career which I have been promoted in, I have stacked up a series of personal self-accomplishments and began to find fulfillment in my professional and personal work. I've written two books, not including this one. One non-fiction and one children's book, including creating the artwork. I've relearned basic application development, I've learned to paint oil on a canvas, I've created and launched a board game, I've started a blog, I've learned about SEO and how to implement it, and most importantly, I've grown as a consultant, a professional and a person. These outputs have increased my fulfillment in my personal work which filtered down to my professional life, again creating a cycle but this time in the right direction.

The most common question I receive from others as I tell them about these successes or when they see my postings online is, "How do you find the time to do all of this?" At first, I struggled for an answer. Maybe it was just that I had more free time and fewer responsibilities than others, but as I continued talking to people and listening to their frustrations, they echoed the same gripes I had experienced just a few years ago. Essentially, the key difference boiled down to how much quality work was being completed in the time we were working. I translated a metric to "real work per minute". If I were to average the amount of real work completed in a single hour and not include time spent checking phones, emails or staring at the screen unsure of what to work on next, it translated to how that time was really being spent and what percentage of it was real work. Even with all my efforts and learnings in place, I am nowhere near a 100% real work ratio in my real work per minute metric, but the small changes have allowed me to accomplish so much more than I had previously been doing.

I've now come to a place of wanting to share my findings and the items that I've seen work for me. They are based on common reoccurring themes that have shown up in my readings on productivity training, mindfulness, motivational guides and an overall search for happiness and value methodologies that can be applied to your daily routine. I only practice 60-80% of my own findings at a time as sometimes life gets away from you and that is ok. Remember, no big and sticky changes occur at once. They take effort and, most importantly, time. Read through this book and start with one small change, one small victory, and then build on it. If something suggested in this book does not work for you, scrap it. Find the items that do work for you and focus on them.

Come and join me at my blog and share your findings and discoveries with us. I look forward to hearing your stories about your transformation into a Mindful Manager and finally getting real work done!

betterment.studio

"Time will pass whether you're using it or not. In five years, you can see the results of your had work, or you can sit there wishing you had started five years ago."

-    Unknown

The Night Before

How you end a day has a significant impact on how you start the next day. By optimizing the last part of your evening, you can begin to plan for success in the morning.

It is no surprise that how we start the day defines what kind of day we are going to have. Someone who hops out of bed excited, organized and ready to execute is probably going to have more of a productive and fulfilled day than someone who snoozes through their alarm, scrambles to get ready and has no idea what the day has in store for them. If you can start your day off right, you are setting yourself up for a lot more successes as the day goes on. Let me first tell you that I am not a morning person. I never have been and, at this point, I'm a fair believer that I never will be. I read every article I could about how to become a morning person or how to set your circadian rhythm to make sure you wake up alert and refreshed. So far, nothing has worked. Not meditation, not avoiding liquids two hours before bed, not removing all screens from my bedroom, nothing.

Waking up, no matter what time it is, has always been one of my greatest weaknesses. Usually self-motivated for most hours of the day, there is something that happens in my brain which zaps me of all my motivation from the moment my alarm goes off until I have brushed my teeth. Once I am past that hurdle, it is smooth sailing. Through talking to others, I found that this is a common problem. Most, like me, just give into the facts and mutter, "I must just be a night owl", shrug and move on.

This caused tremendous frustration for me. As someone who always feels like there is never enough time in the day, wasting the mornings cut deep. Giving into the fact I was not going to be able to change what was happening with my brain and body, I started putting together a plan to just brute force the whole thing.

Buy into The Value of a Good Morning

Take the time to sit down and really accept the value of waking up and having a good morning. Write it down if you need to, as this will help reinforce the idea. This can mean a lot of different things to a lot of different people. For some of us, it is just having some extra quiet time before we really get to work. For others, just some extra undistracted time spent with their families is worth the internal battle to roll out of bed. Some may find value in taking time to knock out emails or creating a daily planner (which we will discuss soon) in order to get a jump start on the day. The key is to be diligent and purposeful with this time. If you plan to spend it scrolling through your phone, then you may have been better off staying in bed.

Start the Good Morning the Night Before

You may not be firing on all cylinders in the morning and that is ok. Stack the odds in your favor by preparing the night before. It is very tempting to skip a lot of minor activities by telling yourself the lie that "you will do it in the morning", but understand that the time spent on the task is not going to change whether you complete it in the morning or the evening prior. All you have introduced are more tasks to complete after you wake up, adding the risk of possibly forgetting something in the morning daze. Sit down and figure out what items you can add to your nighttime routine. Pack your gym bag and put it by the door. Get your pre-prepared meals into the quick grab-and-go containers and stacked in the fridge. Try to find a good balance of being mindful of your morning routine while, at the same time, giving yourself some freedom to run on autopilot as your brain switches on to full capacity.

No Screens in the Room

This means all the screens. No TV, phones or tablets. The blue light emitted from screens has been shown to interfere with the body's natural rhythm. The rhythm is set by the amount of light and dark the body is exposed to called the circadian rhythm. This rhythm is responsible for controlling the timing of many physiological processes such as feeding patterns, brain activity, hormone production, and cell regeneration. When the sun goes down and the world goes dark, the brain begins to release natural sleep hormones into the body like melatonin, which induces sleep. Research has found that the blue light from your devices causes less of these chemicals to be produced at less consistent frequencies, causing us to get a lower amount of sleep at a lower quality.

Set an intention for your bedroom. It is a place of rest and recovery. Do not let the callings of work or the addiction of scrolling through social media interfere with that goal. To ease into this practice, start by no longer placing your phone on the bed stand. Instead, leave it at the opposite side of the room. As you grow comfortable with this distance, graduate to moving the device to the hallway outside your door and so on to the next closest room. Keep going until the phone is at the other end of the home or on another floor. Soon enough, setting your phone down to charge for the night far away from your sleeping quarters will just be part of your routine rather than an anxiety-ridden routine.

For all of this to work correctly, be sure to set the devices to silent before leaving them in another room. Hearing notifications in the middle of the night can not only wake you, but wake the monster inside that begins to whisper anxious thoughts into your head. "Check your phone, it may be something important". Unless you are a life-saving doctor, the chances are that the message you received can wait until the morning during your designated email checking time.

When I started this practice, the worrier in me screamed: "What if there is an emergency in the middle of the night and someone is attempting to reach you for a real emergency?" Most phones have an emergency setting for contact numbers that will override the device's silent settings. If it gives you peace, go ahead and add your close family and friends' phone numbers to this list. If they attempt to contact you in the middle of the night, the device will make an audible alert, waking you.

Set a Bed Time Routine

The biggest killer to a healthy sleep routine is breaking the discipline of keeping the routine. Create a set time for a shutdown routine at the end of the night. Work backward to figure out when this process needs to start. For example, if you set a "lights out time" around 10:30 PM, begin to figure out what time you need to shut down everything in the home to meet that goal, such as flossing or putting the kids down for bed. Set aside time for preparations for the next morning. Tasks like packing gym bags, preparing lunches and putting phones away will take a surprisingly larger amount of time than you may originally think. Once you have created a rough routine and run through it for a few weeks, the process will grow more efficient and quicker as you discover personal tips and tricks that let you speed through with ease. Once you have completed all of the loose ends in and around the home, it's time for the home stretch. Time will be needed to wash up and get settled into bed. Leave some time before lights out for activities that encourage relaxation of the brain. This is a good time to knock out ten or fifteen minutes of meditation or reading.

Tip #1 - Try the body scan meditation technique once you are settled into bed. This begins by scanning slowly from the tip of the head to the toes. Carefully try to notice every inch of the body as you go. Find spots that may be experiencing slight discomfort or spots of tension like the jaw or shoulders. Pause on these areas for a little longer. On every breath out, imagine a little bit of tension leaving the area.

Tip #2 - Reading is highly encouraged during these last few minutes before lights out. Stick to fiction. Let your brain shift into a world-building creative mode as it reads the pages of a book. This is a good time to give the creative part of the brain the last few flexes before you wrap up the day. Avoid non-fiction if possible or books that force you into analysis and comprehension of complex problems. The goal is to bring a state of calm and detachment before bed and this can be counterproductive.

This entire process will require a lot of change, work, and discipline, but do not be too hard on yourself. There is no need to be extremely rigid and stress yourself out in the process as that would be self-defeating. If you run ahead or behind by five to fifteen minutes, no problem. But commit to not staying up hours past your designated lights out time with activities that are not providing value and taking away from the valuable eight or nine hours of rest time needed.

Meal Planning

We all need fuel to get through our day and that fuel comes from the food we eat. With days that feel shorter, our valuable timeslots need to be filled with activities that move you closer to your goals. I understand that for some of you, cooking may serve as a creative and stress-relieving activity, but it can also be extremely time and resource-consuming. Enjoying cooking does not mean you still cannot be a bit more diligent and forward thinking to get the most of your hobbies and your time. Learning to be more strategic with food preparation comes with a series of benefits such as time-saving, better calorie tracking, eating healthier and massive cost savings opposed to eating out for every meal.

Meal planning is the activity of preplanning your entire diet well in advance. If you plan to meal prep, try to plan your meals the weekend before. Create a food board in your kitchen that you can share with your family. A small and simple whiteboard to stick up in your kitchen can be purchased very cheaply. Begin by creating a 3x7 grid on the board. Alongside the left of the board, list out every day of the week. Columns two and three should read 'Lunch' and 'Dinner'. Along the bottom, keep some space to list out items that will be needed from the grocery store.

Example Board:

Meal Plan	Lunch	Dinner
Monday		
Tuesday		
Wednesday		
Thursday		
Friday		
Saturday		
Sunday		

*Shopping List: Bread, Tomato Sauce, Chicken, Milk

As you plan out the week, list out all the items you wish to eat. As you go, check the pantry for the ingredients needed, thus eliminating purchasing extra items, creating waste or spending extra money. The trick to optimizing meal planning is taking what you consume for dinner and parlaying it into a lunch meal. It is also nice to remember to treat yourself from time to time in order to get some variety in case you do not wish to have a reheated lunch every day of the week. Not every meal has to be planned or organized.

Completed Example Board:

Meal Plan	Lunch	Dinner
Monday	Chili	Greek Salad
Tuesday	Greek Salad	Pizza
Wednesday	Pizza	Chicken Enchiladas
Thursday	Chicken Enchiladas	Turkey Burgers
Friday	Turkey Burgers	Work Happy Hour
Saturday	TBD	Dinner with Grandparents
Sunday	PB&J	Chili

*Shopping List: Bread, Tomato Sauce, Chicken, Milk, Broccoli, Fruits, Turkey, Lettuce

Once you have procured all the items you need from the store, set aside time on the weekend to prepare the ingredients. Food preparation is the biggest time-consumer in cooking. Cutting, washing, sifting, and sorting can eat up hours opposed to the time you spend actually cooking and eating the meal. As you put your list together, you will begin to notice overlaps on the ingredients. Get smart about picking foods that share similar ingredients. Begin by getting all the vegetables and sides cleaned and cut for the week in one go. If the items are not needed until later in the week, store them in the freezer and pull them out when needed. You will be amazed at how much efficiency can be gained by grouping similar tasks together and doing them at once. This will ease the washing of cutting boards to just once rather than four or five times. Go ahead and pre-mix your spices and sauces or even cook your larger meals on the weekend and get them stored away for the week. The more you do up front, the most savings you buy yourself during the busy week.

You may need to purchase storage containers from the store if you do not already have them. Once your meals are ready, get them into individual grab-and-go containers. Use smaller containers to separate items. For your lunches, you will want to be able to get them easily in the morning while on autopilot and put them in your lunch bag without much thought.

A significant benefit of meal planning is the cost savings involved and controlling the calories consumed. If done correctly, each meal can cost anywhere between one to two dollars. The savings alone will go a long way opposed to ten-dollar meals each time you eat out. With every prepared meal, it will become easier to control your portions and be significantly healthier than the larger restaurant portions. By eliminating the trip to the car and to the restaurant, valuable time is saved which can be spent on activities such as post-lunch walks to clear your head or other activities you desire. Perhaps a reward of fifteen minutes on social media can happen after your meal!

"The Past does not come with a 'do over' button. But the present does come with a 'do better' button."

- Unknown

Get Eight Hours of Sleep

Besides eating, sleep is the most vital process our bodies crave and require for us to function and be healthy. Getting an adequate amount of quality sleep plays a large role in how efficient we are when we are awake.

The primary benefit of sleep is to give our bodies and brain the rest that it deserves and needs. However, just because we are at rest does not mean we are dormant. While we are asleep, the brain is learning how to adapt to input. It is processing short-term memories and converting them into long-term ones. If we do not get enough healthy sleep, we begin to lose this ability or have it degraded. Memorization and focus become harder during the waking hours and the effort required to retain things increases.

Some researchers also believe sleep may remove toxins from our brains while we sleep. It is known that sleep promotes growth hormones that encourage the healing and repair of cells across our bodies. While at rest, the energy usually required for our active bodies can be diverted to these healing functions instead.

The science is less concrete on the emotional aspects and benefits of sleep but they cannot be ignored. Some believe that sleep is a time for us to process our emotions and to release unwanted feelings. It may be why the advice to "sleep on it" can be so effective to make decisions, as the initial emotions to process what occurs to us may be too volatile to read or act on accordingly. A lack of sleep can trigger or worsen episodes of depression, anxiety, fatigue and put you in a state of general sluggishness during the day. To own the day, you must own the night. Prioritizing healthy sleep will increase your focus and your energy – both vital elements needed to get stuff done.

"We spend so much time being afraid of failure, afraid of rejection. But regret is the thing we should fear most. Failure is an answer. Rejection is an answer. Regret is an eternal question you will never have the answer to."

- Trevor Noah

Starting the Day

The early bird gets the worm. But sometimes the early bird is tired, cranky, unorganized and misses out on getting the good worms if any at all. The first part of your day is the most important. Learn to take steps in the morning to maximize the victories of the day.

Kill the Snooze Button

The snooze button is not your friend. It provides you with a short burst of relief with no longer-term benefits, all while leaving you craving more. If this sounds like a metaphor to drug addiction, that's because it is. To further investigate this, we need to look at what happens when you hit the snooze button.

As the morning hours approach, the brain begins to cycle you back to the shallow states of sleep. This is assuming you have received enough sleep as discussed in the previous sections. When the alarm goes off and the snooze button is hit, a message is sent to the brain, confirming that it is acceptable to go back to sleep. This causes confusion in the brain that can keep you feeling tired throughout the rest of the day. During this time, the brain can usually have strange and vivid dreams. In reality, more time passes than you believe, so you risk sleeping in longer than expected. The truth is, the extra sleep you receive during the extra five minutes does not even count towards making you feel more rested, which ultimately puts you in worse shape. This rough start can lead to drops in productivity and focus throughout the day.

The more and more you hit the snooze button, you begin to create a feedback loop that makes it harder to wake up every successive day. This creates an addition to the snooze button and a more painful jolt when first waking up, making you wish to hit that sweet snooze button one more time.

So, how do we kill the snooze button monster? It is not easy, but the best way to do this is by setting a strict routine. Train the body to know when it is time for bed at the same time every day and every morning. When the alarm goes off, it is time to stretch, groan, curse or whatever it is you need to do to get out of bed. Over time, this will get easier. Your body will learn to adapt to your routine and you will find yourself automatically waking up at the right time. You may not wake up with a pep in your step or become a morning person (I have doubts I ever will), but you will reap many benefits of being up early and on time, making it worth the effort.

If you plan to reward yourself on the weekends with some extra sleep, try not to overdo it and only allow yourself an hour or so of extra sleep. Over time, you will find yourself automatically waking up early as if on your normal routine. One of the most surprising and rewarding experiences for myself was waking up automatically at 8:30 AM on Saturdays and Sundays instead of the 11:00 AM or 12:00 PM I used to. In those quiet hours, I would be able to slowly enjoy my breakfast and coffee and have plenty of time to work on some side projects before lunch. Even a busy body like myself routinely finds himself running out of things to do, but having a clean house and a series of personal projects worked on while still having time for a nice dinner and movie in the evening is a nice benefit to have. There will be late nights on Fridays or Saturdays from time to time, and a single day of breaking routine will not do too much damage, but continually staying up late on the weekends will make it harder to set a routine that you can stick to on the weekends.

Tip - Move your alarm to the other side of the room, out of arm's reach. This will force you to get out of bed and increase the odds of staying out of bed.

Do not use a phone as an alarm. If you have started the practice of not keeping the phone in your room, this will be easier to put into practice. Instead, use a small and simple alarm in the bedroom. The process of having to set it every night is an additional trigger for your brain that it is time for bed and the lights emitted from a small alarm clock are less abrasive than a phone screen.

Early Morning Quick Start

By following the guidelines for the night before, the morning should be a breeze. Meals should be packed and ready to go, gym bags should be by the door and all your clothes picked out. The brain can operate in autopilot for things like brushing your teeth and getting to your car, easing into the day. The precious brain cycles can then be spent on valuable and meaningful activities like enjoying a little time with your family, reading the news or even just a little quiet time.

Morning Mantras and Positive Affirmations

Creating new routines and habits in a short burst and for short periods of time is ordinarily easy, which is why every machine at the gym is occupied in the first few weeks of a new year. However, sticking to routines and making habits stick is a whole different story. This is also why the gym is not as full come February or March. I spent a lot of time researching life hacks to get new habits to stick and become routine. One of the best life hack I found was one that I had written off early on, believing it was not worthwhile. In Eastern cultures, there is a practice of repeating the same phrase over and over, many times in prayer or in a meditative state. These are verbal chants or quiet whispers during the practice. I was not surprised when I saw the recommendation of the practice as I consumed books on Buddhism, mindfulness and other Eastern religions. What caught me off guard was when I began to see the same recommendation in books preaching millionaire success habits or how to increase productivity and fulfillment at work. With what I thought was too much of a coincidence, I attempted the practice and conducted some research and self-experimentation.

What I discovered was that when we pick a mantra and engage in the activity of repeating the phrase to ourselves with focus, we obtain some interesting results. First, our focus is brought directly to the words. The focus is brought to the present, not the future or past, thus increasing the ability to be mindful in the present, something we will discuss in depth a bit later. As our mind focuses, it calms and quiets, creating an exceptional way to start the day. When subjects in a study were tied to functional magnetic resonance imaging (fMRI) as they repeated mantras, the activity being measured was shown to quiet the part of the brain that is responsible for self-reflection and self-judgment.

The sister practice of repeating a mantra is positive affirmations where positive statements are repeated out loud. As we repeat these phrases out loud, there is the reinforcement of the idea in the brain. It has been shown to increase positive emotions, increase self-confidence and set a more defined sense of purpose. On television, you have probably witnessed people pumping themselves up in front of the mirror, repeating phrases such as, "you can do this" or "you're unstoppable". This exercise can be completed at home in the morning before leaving for work. Tell yourself you will have a successful and fulfilling day. Tell yourself that you are kind and loved. Tell yourself whatever it is you need to hear.

What you are witnessing is a positive affirmation being conducted. In contrast to positive affirmations, there are negative affirmations, and unfortunately, for most of us, we cannot control these as easily as we can control introducing positive ones in our thoughts. The brain's default state for many is one of anxiety, natural worries and/or depression. Our thoughts are bombarded with negative affirmations constantly keeping us in a vicious cycle and downfall. With enough discipline, positive affirmations can be used to ward off these negative vibes.

Tip – Obtain a set of meditation or prayer beads, also known as Mala. These are a set of one-hundred-and-eighty beads with a larger stopper bead at one end. When practicing morning mantras, you will not have to worry about keeping count and just focus on the words and their meaning. You can pick a simple mantra such as "om" to repeat or start with. Use your mantra to set your intentions or your goals for the day.

A cheap set of beads can be found online here.

"If you get tired, learn to rest, not to quit."

- Unknown

The Micro To-Do List

Creating a to-do list has always been a go-to practice for productive and successful folks. As a practice, it allows oneself to clear space in their heads for remembering all the small items they need to complete, as well as allowing them to slow down to write items down so they can better plan, schedule and organize these tasks. Once we complete items, we not only free up space on our list, we free up space in our heads. The completed tasks are something we no longer need to worry or think about and we can cross them out.

The problem with a to-do list is that certain tasks can be too high-level or large. They cannot be completed in a short period of time, stretching over a few days or months. Observing the same item on a list over and over and not seeing it go away can have the opposite effect of motivation to complete it. We begin to ignore it. We know it is always there and not something that we must bring to our attention, so instead of chipping away at the task and completing it, we see the task drag out for longer than it needs to, continuing to annoy us and clutter our to-do list.

In addition to having a large to-do list, get in the practice of creating a smaller micro daily to-do list. This list should be created every morning from scratch. On this list, write out the tasks you wish to accomplish just for this day. Nothing more. Try to break these items into time blocks. Add groupings to these items for the morning, afternoon and evening. Once the list is completed, take a moment to shuffle and order as needed from the most difficult to least difficult. As a practice, it is helpful to start with the harder items and then backslide into the easier items before you go to lunch or head home for work. Becoming organized right off the bat in the morning will help you avoid the time lost thinking of what you must do or work on when the time comes. By eliminating this wasteful time spent reorganizing and reprioritizing throughout the day, we can use our time and energy more effectively. Learning how to prioritize and set realistic time frames is a difficult skill to master and will take some time, but with enough practice, you will get better at it. If you have items that were not complete by the end of the day, leave them on your list for the next day. When you start your new list, use the old tasks as a starter for the current day or begin to break them down into smaller chunks if they are too large.

There are many tools and apps available to facilitate this practice, some that gamify the process by giving you points for completing items or even rewarding you for knocking out your punch list. These build on the positive feeling of accomplishment you get for completing a task or even the calm feeling of seeing an empty completed list. As we build on small accomplishments, we create a motivation pattern that allows us to complete larger items. This creates clear and tangible sets of mental rewards that allow us to see the iterative progress towards a larger goal. A feeling that could have been lost without listing, making us lose motivation or purpose.

Tip – Below is one of my checklists as it stands in the state around lunch time. Check out the Mindful Manager app that accompanies this book as it lets you create a simple micro to-do list every day. Use this tool every morning to set your intention for the work items that will get your focus for the day.

To-Do List
- Set up new developer accounts (Afternoon)
- Create POC for Report X (Afternoon)
- Finish Invoices (Afternoon)
- Write Blog Post (Evening)
Completed
- Finish SOW (Morning)
- Test Reports (Morning)

Android
IOS

The Mindful Manager App (Micro To-Do List)

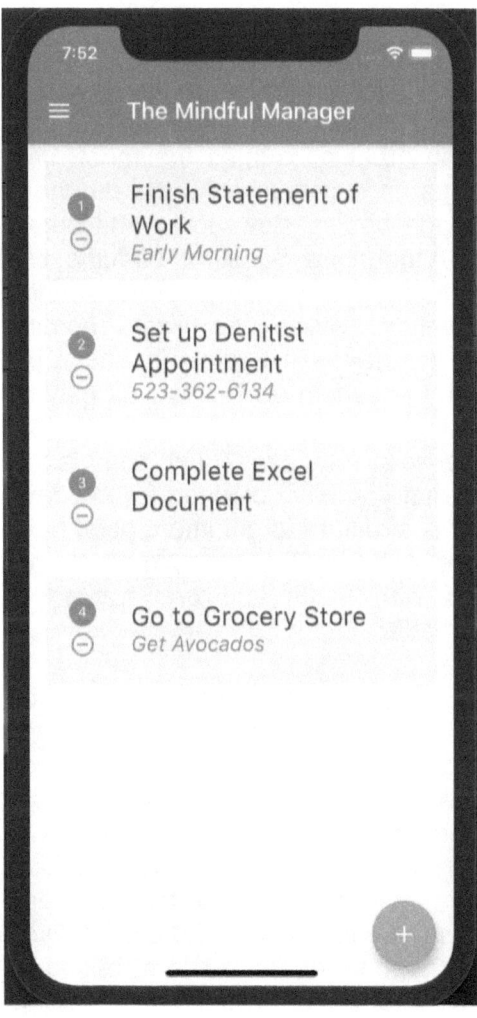

During the Day

Hard Items First

The first task you work on should be the hardest item listed on your micro to-do list for the day. That does not mean the longest or the most tedious item but rather the one that consumes the most brain power and highest in complexity. As the day goes on, our brains and bodies slow down and output can decrease. Although a boost of caffeine can help alleviate this fatigue, it only gives us a short burst of momentum. Utilize the fresh morning energy to start the day with a big win and a big accomplishment. On certain days, this task may be extremely complex and take a long time, and other times it will be relatively easy (just complex in comparison to what you have planned for the day), but still, follow this structure to get into a good habit of doing the hard stuff first. The more you can work on these tasks with focus and undistracted to completion, the better.

Completing large and complicated tasks right off the bat will create a boost of confidence and energy that can be ridden throughout the day, adding on more successes as you go. Look back at your micro-task list organized from the most complex to least complex. When one item is completed, take a few minutes to reset and move on to the next item. Be creative in how you create your list and how you execute it. If you need to reprioritize items based on the time of day, urgency or complexity, go for it. Sometimes the first hour after lunch will be a drag as our bodies are busy expending energy on digestion, so it may be best to pick an activity that suits your energy levels. Everyone has their own flow and process but this method can be used to add a higher level of structure for completing tasks that gradually decreases in mental power to complete.

Some of us suffer from a morning fog, where the brain and body start off feeling slow and have not yet switched off from autopilot mode during the early hours. When arriving at work, park a little further away or take the stairs. Getting the blood flowing through the body will have a positive effect on your general mental alertness.

Tip – The earlier you start your day, the better. Beating others into the office not only provides a nice, quiet and calm environment to start, but it allows you to create your own pace and be less susceptive to interruptions or emails demanding your urgent attention. This will allow for full focus to the first set of complex tasks at hand.

The Five-Minute Checklist

Earlier in this book, we discussed the micro checklist. This was an action item checklist that was focused solely on the items needed for the day. This concept works wonders for larger items of work that can be set aside for blocks of time where you can be heads-down on work items from start to finish in a distraction-free flow. But work, for most of us, is not a series of large tasks that need to be stacked and completed. Littered throughout the day are meetings, phone calls, impromptu fire drills, urgent items that cannot wait or even bathroom breaks and our quick strolls from our desk. This leaves us with smaller blocks of time on our calendars that are too short of a time period to work on any large items and make a significant impact.

This is where the five-minute tasks checklist becomes valuable. This list can be appended to the bottom of your micro to-do list. This is a running checklist of all the small and tiny items that you must take care of during the day that requires less than five minutes of time to complete. Items such as calling the doctor to set an appointment, transcribing the morning meeting minutes, minor non-urgent development tasks or reading an online article you had tagged as important can be added to this list. If you are like me, when you find yourself in a time block between two meetings, the effort of deciding what to do next can be difficult and that time quickly gets wasted surfing the internet. The five-minute tasks checklist now becomes almost a game, trying to complete as many items as I can in the time allotted before I either move to a bigger item or to the next meeting I was invited to. Give this process a shot and you will be surprised by how many tasks on your personal and professional checklist, stagnant for months, begin to get wiped out. You may even find yourself with a completely empty list. If that does occur, take a moment to bask in the stress-free feeling of being at a zero list.

Some may feel guilty about using company time to accomplish small personal tasks, but if you are to step back and really look at how that time would have been spent (randomly surfing the internet, or checking social media which we have all done at work), would you really rate it as quality time spent? In the end, remember to use good judgment and not spend hours of company time on your personal checklist as opposed to your professional responsibilities.

Setting a Timer and Tabata Style Work

What is Tabata? This is one of the most important lessons of the book. It requires a lot of discipline to execute and takes a large amount of time to master the skill. Cal Newport, in the book 'Deep Work', discusses the idea of shallow work and deep work. Deep work is the type of work that creates value and a meaningful product or result. It pushes our brains and makes us really think and work. It is work free from distraction and a maximum utilization of time. In contrast, shallow work is work that is easily repeatable and does not require much intellect. It is sending emails or short burst of menial tasks all the while getting distracted and switching tasks repeatedly.

To be able to accomplish quality deep work, we need to focus on a single task uninterrupted for a significant amount of time. Find a healthy balance between focused work and not overexerting yourself mentally by striving for an hour of work per Tabata session. As you get better, try to push this to two hours. Do not try to push much further than that without giving yourself a chance to get up and move around to rest and reset. The benefits of a small walk will translate to increased gains on a block of time dedicated to working, as opposed to sitting and working for multiple hours on end. We will look at some of the benefits of getting up from your desk in a later section.

Start by picking a single item on your micro to-do list to work on. The list should already be organized and set up during the earlier activities of your morning so that you are not spending too much energy attempting to pick and sort through what item needs attention next. Then, set a timer for one hour and set intentions for this hour. Tell yourself, "I will complete this task", "I will be focused and not get distracted or pulled away". Finally, sit down and get to it. That involves no stopping or taking a break to check your emails, no chatting with coworkers, and no checking your phone for text messages. Just concentrated work. There are many apps and tools that help facilitate this kind of behavior by blocking distracting websites or muting all the colors on the screen to black and white, but most only work to a varying degree of success. The ability to succeed in Tabata style work will come from discipline and effort. Tabata style work will not be easy to master. Like a muscle, every time you break from this routine for even a few days, it will be difficult to come back to it at the same effectiveness it was left at.

Tip - Download the free Mindful Manager app which includes a 1-hour Tabata counter. Select an item to work on, start the timer and go! Nothing fancy about it, just a quick and easy way to start getting work done and learning the habits.

Android
IOS

The Mindful Manager App (Flow Timer)

Find Three Hobbies.

One that makes you money,

One that keeps you in shape,

And one that bring you joy.

Time Blocking

As mentioned earlier, the most common question I receive from others as I've increased the output from my work and my personal projects has been, "Where do you get the time?" I used to struggle with the concept of not having enough time in the past. It always felt as if there were never enough hours in the day and it was impossible to obtain more time without breaking the laws of physics. When I discovered the concept of time blocking through books like Deep Work, Getting Stuff Done and hundreds of articles on Medium, I found a way to begin to get two hours' worth of work done in a single hour. In retrospect, I was really accomplishing an hours' worth of work in an hour, but in comparison to my previous distraction-filled days, I was getting twice as much accomplished.

Building on the idea of Tabata style work and micro to-do lists, focus on getting work organized and grouped into single sets of tasks that can fit into one hour. It may be a single hour-long task, or it may be four fifteen-minute tasks. The goal is to have a group of single-hour work blocks with assigned tasks ready at the beginning of the day. At this point, get time blocks set on your calendar and documented so you can access it easily.

The success of time blocking lies within time blocking the non-work-related items as well. By setting aside time for when we check and respond to emails or taking a walking break, we give our brains the rest and reward they deserve for allowing us to accomplish an hours' worth of focused work. In my opinion, the time blocking method is the most difficult in all of the Mindful Manager processes. Mainly due to technology, we have been trained to respond to every email or message immediately. The next big fire may be happening and require our immediate attention. If we do not respond, we fear repercussions of not appearing to be working or on alert. This mode of operation is usually more detrimental to office productivity as opposed to immediate rapid-fire email replies from one person to the next. Take a moment to reflect on what we are doing when we receive one-sentence emails. We may reply back with a four-word email or forward it to another recipient. Taking a step back and looking at what is happening, you will notice our roles have been reduced to the old 1940's style phone operators. We are just connecting one wire to another all day long, really doing nothing valuable.

I've found that starting a practice of having a set time to read and respond to emails is one that is not easily understood by everyone. Certain types of personalities, with almost a sense of arrogance, believe their emails must be read and reviewed immediately. I suggest not telling anyone you are practicing this methodology and set a five-minute block every hour dedicated to replying to messages. You will be surprised to find that most people will not lose their cool if an email reply does not return in less than fifty-five minutes. Over time, increase the time intervals if possible. It is not unreasonable to expect others to respect your time and allow you to work undistracted as long as you have time set aside for attention to their messages and issues at some reasonable point in time. If something is truly urgent, that message and issue will find its way to you regardless.

Some of us may have roles that support mission-critical tasks. It would not make sense for a doctor to ignore their pager for an hour because they are not in a time block set to reply to messages. In that time, life and death are at play. For roles that require more immediate attention to notifications, create a system of structure outside of work for periods of being on call. Operating in the mindset that all messages must be replied to the second they come in is taxing and detrimental to your long-term mental health and you must strive for a healthy balance where it can be found.

Time is a Construct

Don't worry, this book will not spend time trying to convince you that the idea of time does not exist or that it is all in our minds, but it will ask you to challenge the concept of starting and stopping work at very strict and set times of the day. We discussed time blocking in the previous sections but made no mention that each time block should start either at the top of an hour or at the thirty-minute mark. When getting used to the habit, it may be easier to stick to those thirty-minute intervals, but you will soon find that life does not operate in thirty-minute intervals. Meetings will run early or late, work tasks may take longer than expected or a bathroom break may delay you from starting on a time block exactly at 1:00 PM.

Do not feel restricted to having all blocks of time fit into a set schedule. An hour is an hour no matter when it starts. As we get better at time blocking, we introduce a new stressor to our lives. Living in the idea that we only have eight hours of work to do and a set number of tasks that can fit into those blocks can be uncomfortable. When we ditch the ability to be flexible outside of the thirty-minute intervals, we begin to lose smaller blocks of time that are hidden in our work day. To truly maximize what you accomplish in the day, start with your micro to-do list and begin to shift your thinking. Accept that the value of a day is what you accomplish during the time given vs. how much of the time given you can burn through. As you finish one task, there is no need to wait to move on to the next. Sit back and evaluate where you are physically and mentally. If this is a good time to take a walk or stand up for a minute, go ahead. But if there are twelve minutes left in the hour, that does not mean you have twelve minutes of free time. The next hour of work can start whenever you are ready. This time is also the best time to begin working through your five-minute to-do list.

Get Some Air

We are led to believe that work can only occur while we are seated at our desks, laboring away at one task or another. But quality work should occur away from the desk as well. From time to time, get away from your desk and take a quick walk when time allows. Although it may feel as if tight schedules do not allow for a quick five-minute break, I challenge you to get creative with your schedule. A quick walk can be taken between meetings or when switching tasks. They should be prioritized similarly to your work items. When the CT scans of subjects were compared, the section of the brain showed that going for a walk provides a series of benefits. It lets you take a quick mental break, thus allowing for a sharper mind when returning. While we walk, our brains are free to wander with fewer limitations, letting us work through complex problems and utilizing normally dormant sections of our brains. Like the brilliant and creative thoughts that occur in the shower, walking provides a similar escape from structured thinking executed at the desk and may help you work through complex issues that you may be stuck on. Use this time to think through long-term goals and larger arching work items. Pull out of the tunnel vision of staring at your desk and see the bigger picture. This type of creative thought is just as valuable as the execution of the work and should be prioritized into your day. Adding one small break in the morning and one in the afternoon can be a comfortable place to start.

Additionally, walking comes with health benefits that cycle back to mental health benefits. Studies have shown those who are fitter and more active tend to have a better overall quality of life which extends to the workplace. This additional benefit can divert issues like pains and illnesses and have direct correlations to how successfully you execute all day. With two quick walks scheduled into a day and work out in the morning or evening, it is easy to achieve your health goals while having a successful career and personal life.

Taking a break from your desk does not mean we spend hours gossiping and talking by the water cooler or hallway. How we spend our mental break time should be purposeful and tactful. It is easy to waste this time and then be caught working late, thus throwing off your routine and losing valuable time that could be used more effectively.

Focus on What You're Good At

For those ambitious types, it is easy to say yes to all work that comes your way. You may even feel like it is your professional responsibility to agree to all work that is thrown at you. There is an interesting concept that came up repeatedly during my research and writings by different authors. There is a commonality of teachings suggesting to focus and work on only the things you are good at and delegate or offload the work you are not.

First, let's dive deeper into the work you do not want to do or are not good at. This work may simply be work you do not enjoy or doesn't bring happiness and value to your day. Take a moment to list out the activities that consume your time and really think about what is on your plate, and whether or not you really need to be the one that does that work. Does it make sense to offload that work? Can you hire a temp or even train a junior resource to take that item off your plate and free you up for more quality, valuable, fulfilling work? The effort you put into these tasks is lackluster if your heart is not quite in it. There will always be grunt work or some task you have to complete because it is your responsibility. I don't believe your wife is going to be happy if you bring a stranger into the house to clean the dishes, but possibly investing in a dishwasher can free up thirty minutes of your night. If that time is spent in quality time with your significant other or working on a personal growth project, then the value is easy to see.

Next, let's look at what happens when you work on items you are good at or really enjoy. You lose time and you breeze through the tasks. You feel a sense of joy and accomplishment. There are tangible benefits to this work. Benefits for yourself and the other recipients of your output. You work faster than others that don't enjoy a similar task, and you produce higher quality work because your passion is in it. By effectively removing the low-quality tasks and using that time for high-quality, we obtain very real benefits. If you spend thirty dollars to have someone mow your lawn, a task you may hate, ask yourself, can you spend that new-found time working on a project that may make you thirty thousand dollars down the line? If you take an hour a day to train a junior at work on tasks that normally just take you fifteen minutes a day, then the ROI will be returned in just four days. After that point, you consistently have free time that was never previously available to you. Find the items you are great at and enjoy and focus on those. Being an expert at just a few things is much more valuable than being ok at a lot of things.

"Meditate on this…Don't start your day with broken pieces of yesterday. It will definitely destroy your today and ruin your great tomorrow"

-    Rza

Killing the Notifications

While in the midst of my frustrations about work, my typical days had begun to take on a familiar routine. Get to work at eight and grab a coffee while my computer started up. I would sit down and parse through the emails I had not looked at on my phone as I had gotten ready in the morning. Once complete, this was followed by a small exercise of trying to figure out what I was supposed to work on and surfing the internet. After some wasted time, I finally got down to work. I would work for about ten minutes before my email notification would pop up. Something unsubstantial, but my work would be put on pause as I would answer all emails right away. It even earned me the reputation of being a hard worker. I would then shift back to what I was doing. What was I doing again? Oh, yeah…that's right. Back to work. Ten minutes wasted. Five minutes into work, the email notification would chime again. This time, it would be a follow-up question to my previous email. Again, stopping all that I was doing, the email would be responded to, followed by a quick check of the internet and then a shift back to work. Five minutes of work, another notification. This time, it is a text message. Nothing important but I reply anyway. I try to get back to work but am immediately interrupted by another email notification. Just an email to say "thanks" for my previous reply. Attention diverted again. Back to work.

As the morning rolled on, I am interrupted by social media notifications, text messages, email notifications, a software update, and a meeting alert. Looking at my calendar, it is time for lunch. Looking at my screen, I realize I have not finished the task I had started in the morning that really should have only taken about forty-five minutes to complete.

If you're like me, just reading this should give you anxiety as you self-reflect on your similar days and nights. The notifications from our applications scream for our attention and pull us away from the task we should be focusing on in the present. "cite study"

Open Office, Closed Office

When the second big technology boom occurred in the early 2000s, companies such as Google and Facebook expanded their workforces at remarkably quick rates. Their office spaces grew as they filled them with the best engineers, developers, and business people in the world. While trying to accommodate all of their staff and create new workspaces that fostered a culture, cooperation, knowledge sharing, and rapid development, a new type of workplace was created that had not quite existed or been popular before. The end of days loomed for the rows and rows of high-walled cubicles, with employees crammed into five-by-five work compartments. This was where the open office was born. On a 60-minute episode, companies flaunted their vast one-room giant office. Shared tables and benches replaced cubicles. Developers worked on beanbag chairs and conference rooms became giant transparent fishbowls. These ideas caught on like wildfire and, nowadays, most companies have some version of an open office for their employees to work in.

As these office design principles became the norm, it felt as if no one stopped to think about the negative aspects of what such an environment could create. Yes, collaboration was encouraged by being able to lean over or walk over to a coworker and discuss a problem or an issue. No one stopped to think about the time lost to stop what that coworker was doing, mentally having to switch gears to answer the question and then come back to the task they were working on. With the distraction already happening, the coworker then spends some time checking emails or the internet before trying to get back into work. It is said that it takes fifteen minutes to get back into a workflow, and within those fifteen minutes, that person is interrupted again. Whether it is another tap on the shoulder, or a loud conversation across the hall, or people shuffling by, the mind is quickly drawn to the attention-seeking event and flow is broken again. White noise from the office or from folks in the breakroom or the daily stand-ups in the open area further propagating the problem.

So, what is the solution to the ever-popular open office? It is not like we can demand our bosses or CEOs to undergo an expensive reconstruction to facilitate our needs and build us our own private cubicles. I've found personal success in creating a virtual cubicle when in these situations. First, eliminate the noise. Invest in a good pair of noise

canceling headphones, preferably rechargeable or purchase rechargeable batteries.
More Material

Clear the Clutter and Embrace Minimalism

A cluttered life creates a cluttered mind and a cluttered mind cannot think clearly. Take a look around you. At your work station, your desk, in general rooms you hang out in or live in. Take stock of as many items as you can, no matter how small. Take note of larger items like furniture and your computer to small things like a loose paper clip or basic stationery. How many of these items did you use last week? Last month? In the last six months? The chances are, there are some if not a lot of items you can either discard or can be put away in some place that is out of sight and out of mind. It is no secret that having lots of objects and a messy environment creates a stress-inducing environment for the brain. Nothing is more therapeutic than a good old-fashioned purge. Evaluate if you really do need items or if they are something you can part with. There may be a strong urge inside of you that screams, "I need this", but I encourage you to challenge that voice. The items that provide little value and take up valuable space in your life and may be useful to someone else. Sell it, donate it, give it away. Whatever it takes. The next time you are about to impulsively purchase an item, really ask yourself the same question. Will this item bring value to my life? If it does, go ahead and add it to your collection.

Decluttering goes for your computer desktop as well. A cluttered and messy computer desktop will eat at your soul in the same way a cluttered physical desktop will. As we move into the digital cloud age where storage has grown at a massive rate with the cost falling in-line, it is easy to never have to delete a file again. But what good is that file if it can never be found or if it really never was needed?

Create a routine at a healthy cadence to move files to accurate folders and scan those folders for what can be purged. The professional inside of you will ask, "But what if I need this file for later?", but do not become a digital hoarder. Keep what is important and what you are sure will be used again. All files with four rows of data that you have not opened in a year, titled 'book(4).csv' can and should go in the recycling bin. In fact, challenge yourself to only have one icon on your desktop and keep the recycling bin empty as well. There is no point in gaming the system by clearing the files, knowing you have a safety net of a thousand files in the recycling bin that are ready to recover.

Single Tasking, Not Multitasking
Many times, our egos get the better of us. Our confidence in being able to work on multiple items at once is grossly inflated. We feel that working on multiple articles while keeping up with our phones and emails and simultaneously eating is a skill we have mastered and are capable of doing flawlessly. We believe doing many things at once lets us

produce multiple pieces of work in a condensed period of time. This is a big lie. Multitasking is not as advantageous to our success as believed. The human brain is not capable of working on multiple tasks at once as it was not designed to multitask. When you multitask, there is no deep, meaningful work being completed. The work is shallow, mindless and probably not of much value. Realistically, the work items being completed are taking longer than the true time it should have taken.

MIT neuroscientist, Earl Miller, notes that our brains are "not wired to multitask well… when people think they're multitasking, they're actually just switching from one task to another very rapidly. And every time they do, there's a cognitive cost."

When we multitask, at the neurological level, our brain is hit with a quick shot of dopamine every time we complete a small tiny task. This includes non-value tasks such as replying to an email, a quick check of your social media or answering a text message. For a microsecond, we are hit with dopamine and the feeling of gratification. This begins the additional cycle of wanting to multitask more and more. Multitasking has also been found to increase the production of cortisol, the stress hormone. More mental clutter and more stress lead to things such as lower memory retention power, a harder time focusing and an overall decrease in mental health.

The quality of our work is what suffers the most. We no longer produce anything large or meaningful. We feel as if our perception to others depends on appearing busy and consumed, but underneath it all, our value decreases. The expectation must be set in today's workforce that being a multitasker is not a skill to brag about, but rather a large flaw in how we live our lives and work effectively. As hard as it may be, we must learn to work on one item at a time and give it the attention it deserves to be completed successfully and to the best of our ability.

Tip – Remember to try the focus timer in the Mindful Manager app the next time you are working. Try to work on just one item for as much of the hour as possible. Fight the temptation to check your phone or email or have your attention diverted to anything but that task. This may prove to be difficult, but over time, it becomes easier as you go.

Android
IOS

Flow

As you begin to learn how to work efficiently and efficiently, it will be easy to lose track of time. Minutes and hours will zoom by without even realizing it while in the state called "flow". In positive psychology, a flow state, also known as being in the zone, is the mental state of operation in which a person performing an activity is fully immersed in a feeling of energized focus, full involvement, and enjoyment in the process of the activity. In essence, flow is characterized by complete absorption in what one does, and a resulting loss in one's sense of space and time.

Named by Mihály Csíkszentmihályi in 1975, the concept has been widely referred to across a variety of fields, though the concept has existed for thousands of years under other names, notably in some Eastern religions.

Achieving a state of flow is the greatest superpower one can have in today's world and workforce. This state is what will allow you to complete two or three hours' worth of work in one. With no distractions pulling your attention away, every precious second will be dedicated to just one single task. It is through this kind of hyper-focus that you will be able to complete large amounts of work and feel a true sense of accomplishment.

Brainwaves and Music. Good Noise and Bad Noise

When achieving a state of flow, the audible sounds we hear play a large role in either helping dive deeper into the state or pull us out completely. Different sounds can affect us differently. When we are working, loud conversations or sounds jar us back to the world around us and break our concentration. It can take up to five minutes to regain that concentration again once it is lost. As music enters the ear, it engages many different areas of our brains, some of which are used for other cognitive functions. Low noise levels apparently get our creative juices flowing, whereas in high noise levels, our creative thinking is impaired because we're overwhelmed and struggle to process information efficiently.

Music and sound can play a great role in helping achieve maximum concentration and focus. Research suggests that ambient noise, or ambient music, could be the best kind of music for work productivity. Ambient music without lyrics has also been shown to be the most effective for when trying to retain new information. Music with lyrics, on the other hand, seemed to have the opposite results. Music with lyrics can create enough distraction to limit intense focus, but when it came to the mundane or repetitive task, music with lyrics was shown to help as it provided relief from the boredom of the chore.

"Sometimes the smallest step in the right direction ends up being the biggest step in your life. Tip toe if you must, but take the step"

-    Unknown

After Work

Shutting Down

As the workday ends, a new phase of the day begins. In the same way as employees are expected to not engage in too many non-work-related activities while on the company clock, you owe it to yourself to not engage in too many work-related activities during your personal time. The value and protection of this time must come from within. If you do not respect it, others won't either. If others know you are "always on", then work-related items will find their way to you at all hours of the day. If you wish to have time for yourself, whether it is to spend on your own, with your family or on side projects, then none of those will benefit by blending work-related items into those precious hours.

As the day ends, create a routine that signals to the brain and the body that the work day is over. By working at top capacity throughout the day with focus, there should be no reason to take work home with you frequently. Certainly, in this day and age, working from home will occur from time to time, but considering this as the norm and stretching workdays to twelve hours a day, seven days a week is not healthy. At the end of the day, review your micro to-do list. Observe which items were completed and cross them out. Allow a moment to feel satisfied with yourself. Next, look at the items still remaining on the list and reassess what the next day looks like. It is a good idea to get a jump on tomorrow's list by getting three to four items penciled in. This will save some time in the morning instead of racking your brain on where you had left off the previous day.

Tidy up your workspace before you leave and clear up any clutter that may have been created. Put everything back in its rightful space and throw away any trash. For your computer, many people just switch the machine to hibernate or sleep mode so that they may pick up exactly where they left off. This can create a sense of work in flight or unaccomplished tasks that linger in your thoughts. If at all possible, shut down applications and the computer. It will force you to stop and think about where things are ending for the day and making sure items are saved correctly. A good restart is usually healthy for a computer as it will give some of the components a break and allow temporary cached files and software in memory to be flushed so the computer can function better the next time it is booted up.

Healthy Body, Healthy Mind

Over and over, I have committed myself to different workout routines and diets in an attempt to get in my ideal shape. Some regiments worked to certain degrees and others not so much. I created a spreadsheet to track my calories and began eating well. In addition to this, I started to complete high-intensity workouts twice a week and lifting weights twice a week. Over a ten-month period, I had lost twenty pounds, I was the strongest I had ever been and could do cardio longer than I had previously been able to. Thinking I had discovered a miracle routine, I shared my new secret routine with a friend. His reply, "So, you're telling me that if I eat clean and workout consistently, I will get in shape and lose weight? Wow, surprising".

He was right. I had discovered what had been known for centuries. There was no need for special diets or training routines. Just being mindful of the food I put in my body and mindful of how I expended my energy was all it took.

Keeping a healthy body is the Ying to the Yang of a healthy mind. Both need to be nurtured in balance to truly be in a happy state. There is no need to deep dive the benefits that exercise has on the body. That has been well-documented throughout time. However, it is important to explore the benefits it has on the mind. Exercise increases blood flow in the body which aids in the release of hormones that participate in creating a healthy environment for the growth of brain cells. It can stimulate new connections between brain cells in different parts of the brain. In a study done at the University of British Columbia, researchers found that regular aerobic exercise, the kind that gets your heart and your sweat glands going, appears to boost the size of the hippocampus – the brain area involved in verbal memory and learning.

Exercise has also shown to help lower stress, anxiety and help combat depression. It can increase energy levels throughout the rest of the day and help with your mood. Many studies have suggested that the parts of the brain that control thinking and memory (the prefrontal cortex and medial temporal cortex) have greater volume in people who exercise versus people who don't.

When it comes to the act of working out, the type of exercise does not quite matter. To get the benefits of exercise, it is recommended to engage in both cardio as well as resistance training to obtain a well-rounded workout and maximize your health gains. For cardio, try engaging in HIIT (High-Intensity Interval Training). HIIT is a form of interval training, a cardiovascular exercise strategy alternating short periods of intense anaerobic exercise with less intense recovery periods. HIIT will get your heart rate up faster and longer than steady state cardio. In addition to the shorter length of workouts, HIIT will provide the benefit of an after-burn calorie expenditure effect, lasting long after the workout.

When trying to get in shape, it is easy to just commit to cardio and skip the weights. Resistance training is an important part of keeping your body healthy. Not only will you put valuable muscle mass that can help with posture, pain, balance and a slew of other benefits, but muscles also continue to burn calories while at rest. A single pound of muscle is a fraction of the physical size of a pound of fat, so do not worry about looking too bulky.

Keep an eye out in your day for quick health breaks. Park a bit further down from your office and get some extra steps in. Take the stairs instead of the elevator. Get up and take walking breaks where they fit in your schedules. Very little effort will go a long way in the long run. The healthier your body gets, the sharper you will find your mind. Other items in your life should become a little easier and hopefully a little happier. Remember, no one has ever regretted a workout, but everyone has regretted skipping one.

Meditation

Meditation ranks as the most important skill one can learn. Also called mindfulness, living in the now or being present, the idea of meditation was heavily prevalent in all my reading and research. As expected, it appeared as the primary skill in books on Eastern philosophies and religions. Recently, it has gained immense popularity in the West as a tool for combating stress, anxiety, and depression. Online articles on the practice can be found by the thousands on popular blogs and are now prevalent in the startup scene. In books geared towards success, happiness and finding purpose, meditation was not always listed as a primary topic, but concepts such as being present, creating positive energy with your body and thoughts or learning to focus were always a common theme. In the books written by success life coaches, I was not sure if the authors had realized it or not, but they were essentially preaching meditation and mindfulness techniques to their reader in most of their tips and tricks.

Meditation has shown to have a series of mental and physical benefits. When paired up with the physical exercise, it is a powerful tool for finding a calm that translates to your professional and personal success. Below are just a few benefits of meditation. With enough practice, you can begin to increase your sense of wellbeing and control your emotions.

1: Meditation reduces stress
Meditation is incredibly effective at reducing stress and anxiety. One study found that mindfulness and Zen-type meditations significantly reduce stress when practiced over a period of three months. Another study revealed that meditation literally reduces the density of brain tissue associated with anxiety and worrying.

2: Meditation increases your sense of well-being
Mindfulness meditation increases your psychological functioning and, in the process, improves your sense of well-being. Yoga and tai chi have been found to do this as well. According to studies, they have significant therapeutic effects and increase the quality of life when practiced regularly.

3: Meditation increases your sense of connectedness and empathy
Loving-kindness meditation (sometimes called Metta) is a compassion-based meditation that enhances brain areas associated with mental processing and empathy. It also increases your sense of social connectedness.

4: Meditation improves focus

Research shows that meditation improves cognition and increases your ability to perform tasks requiring focus.

5: Meditation improves relationships
Meditation has been shown to better your ability to relate to others. It improves your ability to empathize and sharpens your ability to pick up on cues indicating how others are feeling. Meditation also increases your emotional stability, making you less likely to be influenced by any negative people in your life.

6: Meditation makes you more creative
According to certain studies, meditation increases your creativity. Allowing the brain to quiet all of the outside commotion and distractions, we may be able to tap into our existing creativity hidden behind all the noise.

7: Meditation improves memory
Research has shown that meditation improves your ability to memorize information and to store and consolidate it efficiently.

8: Meditation improves your ability to make decisions
High-powered executives turn to meditation to help them do their jobs better. Studies have found that mindfulness meditation helps you make better decisions by improving the functioning of your brain's decision-making centers.

9: Meditation helps you find "flow"

The mental state called "flow" is a rare state where the human mind is operating in complete harmony with itself when you reach a challenge perfectly suited to your abilities. Meditation can help you reach this amazing state of mind, according to some fascinating research.

10: Meditation reduces physical and emotional pain
Meditation has the capability to reduce mental and physical pain better than certain drugs.

Tip – You do not require expensive tools, furniture or appliances to meditate. All you need is a quiet, comfortable place to sit. Begin with 10 minutes a day and increase the time as you grow more comfortable.

1.   Find a comfortable place to sit. If sitting on the floor is too uncomfortable, find a chair or even your sofa. No location is wrong for a beginner meditator.

2.   Begin with your eyes open and breathe in deeply. Four seconds in, hold for two seconds and then exhale for four seconds. Repeat these three times. Close your eyes on the third breath.

3.   Begin with a body scan. Start scanning the body from top to bottom very slowly, moving down with the breath. Focus on every inch as you go. Notice your earlobes, your elbows, your shins. Notice the parts of your body that normally do not get a millisecond of your attention during the day. Pause for longer on parts of the body that may feel tight or tense, such as your jaw or shoulder. With every exhale, release some tension from that part of the body.

4.   Once you reach the bottom of your body in your scan, bring the attention to the breath or the point between your eyebrows. Hold this focus and feel the body expand and contract with every breath. Stay in this moment for as long as you can.

5. Thoughts will come and attempt to pull you along with them. This is natural. Once you realize you have drifted, note it, forgive yourself and return the breath slowly.

6. Keep with this pattern until the timer rings.

To help make this practice easier, we have included two features in the Mindful Manager app. The first is a simple breathing tool which can be used at any part of your day to focus your breathing. Take a few long breaths between tasks to center yourself and bring your mind back to a state of calm. The second is a meditation timer. This can be used by beginner meditators to learn ten-minute meditation without having to worry about keeping track of time. Just find a comfortable place to sit, set the timer and get going.

Android
IOS

The Mindful Manager App (10 Minute Mediation)

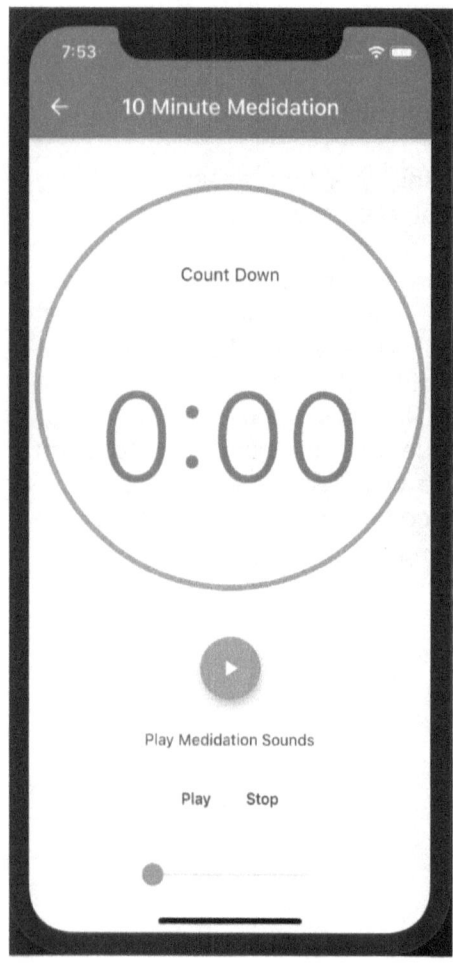

No Zero Days

Stuck to the back of my door in my study is a hand-drawn sign. The sign reads "No Zero Days". I found this mantra at one of the lower points in my life. I was frustrated, feeling useless and unfulfilled. As I exacerbated my problems by surfing the web, I came across a blog of a similar name to this section geared towards helping folks at a level of depression so bad, they could not get out of bed to take a shower, clean their room or workout. Doing any meaningful hobbies or learning something new was out of the question completely. The primary message of the blog was to never have a zero-day. A day where you do nothing. Even it if was one small thing such as taking a shower, doing twenty-five jumping jacks or unloading the dishwasher, it counted as successfully having avoided a zero-day.

Compounding this with creative writing productivity tips I had been reading about, there was a common suggestion designed to help defeat procrastination or writer's block. It suggested to force yourself to sit down and just write two sentences. That's it. Even if you were facing critical levels of writer's block, it was easy to process the idea of being able to crank out two sentences of writing. What usually happened afterward was that the two sentences turned into a few hundred.

The hardest hurdle of procrastination is the initial sitting down and getting to work, not the work itself. Even if you are only able to write two sentences before you hit a wall, that little bit of work moves you closer to your goals of writing a blog post or a book that did not exist a short while ago. This method translates to more than just writing. Any work or side project can be given five minutes of your time in the evening. Maybe it is the painting you are working on, or maybe it is the online class you are enrolled in. By promising yourself you will not have a zero-day and will take at least one small step towards your goal, you will one day look back at the mountain of growth accomplished.

It is important to look at what procrastination is and how it affects us. We all suffer from it and are guilty of giving into it. Procrastination at its core is an avoidance of pain and fear. At some subconscious level, we feel that the task we should be working on is going to bring us some level of discomfort. We may feel it is boring or difficult, so we avoid the task by putting it off. By doing this, we only delay the negative feelings that are coming our way regardless. Most of the time, what we fear is not as bad as it is in reality. Emptying the dishwasher or cleaning your room is quite a rewarding experience once complete and not extremely difficult or painful to accomplish. Still, that tiny part of our brains wants us to put off the task by telling us there are more desirable things to be doing such as scrolling through your phone or watching more television. The next time you are struggling with this voice in your head, tell yourself this is a no zero-day moment. Pause what you are doing and put away a few dishes, or agree to study for five minutes. Start off slowly, and hopefully, it will translate to more positive work than you originally planned for.

Tip - It may help to give that little voice in your head a name. Something to identify the procrastination and negative thoughts by. By creating a mental separation of knowing the voice is not the true you, it will give you something to argue with and attempt to conquer.

If You Must Work

Sometimes there is no avoiding it. Critical work comes up in the nights and weekends. You have a responsibility to yourself and to others that must supersede your own personal time. With the tips and tricks learned in this book, it should be easy to minimize how often this occurs but it is not completely unavoidable in the modern workforce. When work does pop up after-hours or during the weekend, treat it like a targeted action item. Take a moment to think on the task and determine what the task is, what work is entailed and how long it will take. Once you have taken stock of what is required, plan the work in a set time block that does not interfere too wildly with your routine. It could be in the hour directly after dinner or possibly after your post-work workout. Try to avoid making it the last thing you do before transitioning to your nighttime shut down routine. Transitioning from work directly to sleep does not give enough mental separation from the end of one workday to the beginning of the next, leading to mental exhaustion and burn out. Create a gap to read or decompress once the work item is complete, sending a signal to the brain that the workflow of the current date is separate from the next.

Sleep

At the beginning of this book, we discussed the importance of getting quality sleep. Not to belabor the point, but plan to get a minimum of eight hours of sleep. This means wrapping up work, television, phone surfing, side projects, and housework at a reasonable time so that you may begin your bedtime routine. When we let these tasks linger too close to bedtime, they find their ways into our thoughts and dreams, leaving us with uncomfortable rest. Give meditation or reading fiction a try as one of the last activities you do before bed to force the mental slow down needed for sound sleep.

"Don't live the same year 75 times and call it a life"

- Robin Sharma

Skills and Life Hacks

Focus

Being able to focus is a critical skill to success. Without the ability to give a single task a hundred percent of your attention, completing that task cannot be done quickly, efficiently or to the best of your ability. Being able to commit to one hour of work or even having the discipline to sit down and create a micro to-do list takes focus. It is the foundation for the success of everything listed in this book so far.

The ability to focus is a skill. It can increase and be elevated with diligent work and practice or it can atrophy over time without the proper care. To make matters worse, with modern technology attempting to pull us into multitasking or digesting micro news stories on the internet, this accelerates the decrease of the ability to focus on a single task for a reasonable time. Like a muscle, the brain must be worked-out consistently to stay strong and sharp. Below are a few changes you can begin to make to help bring your ability to focus to the next level.

1) Read

Every few months, an article reading "All successful people do this one habit every day" shows up on one of my feeds. At this point, I know what exciting secret the article is hiding and wanting to share. It is reading. People like Bill Gates, Warren Buffett and President Obama admit to reading at least one hour a day, seven days a week. By adopting this habit, in addition to being a forever learner and growing your knowledge, reading engages you in an activity that demands 100% of your attention to complete. It is impossible to read and multitask. With a book, there are no other links to jump to, or notifications pulling for your attention. The type of reading you do does not need to be solely non-fiction either. Fiction can pull your attention so deep that you forget you are reading words on a page as your brain plays out the theater of the story in your mind. This balance between focus and creativity can be a Zen-like state for most.

2)   Cut the phone, Internet and media scrolling

The invention of the smartphone and the applications that followed gave us some of the greatest tools we know today, but they also created a new consumption frenzy that has been very detrimental to our mental and emotional health. The battle between a constantly distracted life and mindful focus is raging on in our heads and most of us are either losing the battle or unaware we are fighting for the wrong side. As I wrote this section of the book, I was two hours into a four-hour flight for work. I recalled a time just a few years ago, when the plane was one of the last few safe places that we were forced to disconnect from our devices and turn to our hobbies of old, which seemed to find less and less time on our priority lists while on the ground. Things like reading, internet-less writing, really listening to music or even the simple task of staring out the window and daydreaming. Nowadays, most flights provide Wi-Fi once you cross the ten-thousand feet range. I looked around and like junkies waiting for a fix (myself included), passengers sat with phones in hand waiting for the seat belt light to shut off so they could connect to the free network the airline provided. With most airlines now ditching in-seat screens and forcing passengers to use their own devices to stream media, for those first twenty agonizing minutes, passengers were truly unplugged. Some resorted to quick swipe games. A quick hit of the soft drugs before they could get back on the data mainline.

Once the plane crossed the ten-thousand feet altitude mark, chaos struck. The network was unavailable. Passengers turned to one another asking, "is the internet working for you?" After confirming it was not just a nightmare happening to them and attempting several phone restarts, the call service lights began to "ding" throughout the plane. Passengers asked the flight attendants if and when the network would return, to which they were told the awful news that the internet was not going to be available during this flight. Unfortunately, sometimes technology does not work the way it's supposed to. I am also a current addict working to get a better handle on my technology addiction. Like an Alcoholics Anonymous member, I've at least accepted I have a problem and am trying to cut back. As I sat back and watched the last thirty minutes unfold, I decided it would be a good time to document what was occurring and what the core issue was.

When social media went mainstream in the early 2000s, it created a way to connect people across the globe at a previously unprecedented rate.

Platforms such as Facebook, Twitter, and Reddit have accumulated massive userbases under free registrations. But the end game was not to create the network, it was to monetize them and it was achieved under the umbrella of advertising as Google had once done. The ability to target advertisements to users has marketers flocking to tech companies like Facebook to publish their advertisements, which Facebook happily obliges...for a cost, of course. Social media companies then get their algorithms to figure out what ads to show at the right times. They provide value to their real customers (the marketers) by ensuring ads get seen and convert to clicks and leads via user engagement. Their primary goal is to obtain as much of your time as possible looking at their app. Cramming in dog food ads while you look at cute puppy videos, or meal delivery services when you Google search "what is the Keto diet?" The ultimate goal for these companies is to pull your already short attention away from the real world and back to your devices.

This is where the brilliant creation of notifications and "likes" became the new crack. Our devices started to gently alert us of small interactions on each of the platforms. Each one screaming, "hey, look over here for a second, will ya?" Researchers discovered that quick updates and checking of the notifications created a micro dopamine spike in the brain. After a series of hits, the brain begins to create an addiction cycle. Users begin checking their phones even if there is not a notification present and begin mindlessly scrolling through their feeds for anything that may give them the little kick their brain is asking for. During this time, ads are being fed with every swipe and scroll while your long-term attention span decreases.

Netflix and streaming services, while not classified as social media, are in the battle for your attention as well. Assuming you are sleeping for eight hours and at work for eight hours, that leaves eight hours of free time and you better believe Netflix wishes to claim every last second of that time. It is why they have invested millions of dollars in content. It is why they let you skip the introduction and credits of the show. Just roll right into the next episode and facilitate the "binge" watch. The healthy and normal one-hour you dedicated to unwinding quickly turns into three hours.

Social media and streaming apps are not the only culprits in the shortening of our attention spans. We also have mobile games. This is a sensitive topic for me personally as I grew up a gamer. I always enjoyed deep story-driven games, but taking a look through the top-selling games on the app stores, most games only require a few swipes or taps to play. Between each round of the same patterns, advertisements and microtransactions are served to the users. Reviews read "great time killer" which makes you ask yourself, why are we trying to kill time? Our most precious commodity. The only commodity you can only expend and never accumulate.

Our devices and the applications we run on them refuse to allow us to focus on any one thing for a significant period of time. As time goes on, we find ourselves missing out on our family and friends as we look at our phones during dinner. Our work output and job satisfaction decrease. Our happiness and contentedness, like the frog in boiling water, slowly decrease without us being aware. We are no longer mindful of what is happening around us and instead of actions scientifically proven to make us feel better like gratitude and human connection, they are replaced by "likes" and "friend requests" to people you will never speak to in real life. Outdoor activities that replenish your vitamin D and spike your serotonin become far and few between as scrolling through Reddit and Instagram are your new connections to the outside world. Silicon Valley has successfully pulled us out of the present moment and is investing big dollars into new ways to keep our flow broken.

It's easy to document the issue but figuring out where we are and where we need to get back to is not an easy task. Looking around the plane, deeper self-realization of my own problem became more apparent and I tried to shut down my laptop for a moment to sit still and observe as I used to as a child. Within five minutes, the need to open my phone or computer began to brew in me. I tried my ten-minute meditation routine but there was too much noise on the plane to focus. What finally calmed me was looking out the window to see the sun setting on Scottsdale, Arizona. The sky transitioned from yellow to a dark red in almost a picturesque image and, finally, the little voice screaming to open my phone faded as I shifted into a good old-fashioned daydream. For the first time since the flight took off, I felt my anxiety drop, a small validation that this new mental state was a healthier place for me and all of us. The realization of the goal and the comprehension of the problem seemed like a good first step but I just hope that, over time, the discipline to move to a more mindful place has a fighting chance against all the companies wishing to crush it. Only time will tell.

3)   Meditate
The benefits of meditation and how to meditate have already been outlined in this book. Take time daily to work on the practice. With every session, get better at holding the attention on the breath. This focus will strengthen over time.

4)   Flash Cards and Puzzles
There is no need to download a fancy app for brain games. An easy low-cost way of giving your brain a quick workout is by creating a set of flash cards like the ones we used to have when we were young. Start by taking a piece of paper and drawing a simple 10x10 grid. Label each square from 1 to 25, repeating each number twice as shown in the example below. Cut the squares out and there you have it, simple matching flashcards. Scramble them up and flip them over. The point of the game is to find matching cards and remove them from the pile until complete. To make more of a game of it, time yourself each time and try to beat your score every

few days. As time goes on and your focus and memory grow stronger, you will get faster at completing the game.

Home Made Sample Cards

Another fun way to work out your brain is to do puzzles. Crosswords, Sudokus or Word Searches will do the trick but you can also take up chess or other board games if you have a friend available to play with you.

5)   Be Creative
When we enter kindergarten, we are given crayons and pencils and colorful paper and we are told to create. We are encouraged to imagine and experiment. By the time we enter high school, creative writing in English class is all that is left from mandatory art classes. By college, if you are not majoring in the arts, our class work gives us

little to no exposure to the creative activities we once started with.

When we enter the current workforce, recruiters search for "rock stars" or "masters of their craft". They search for candidates with "passion" who can "build creative solutions for their business challenges". Being hardworking and logical will always be an essential skill for all companies, but most are always hunting for the unicorns. The ones that can adapt, imagine, enhance and solve complex problems that require more than just brute force. If being creative is such an important and valuable business skill, then why is it stripped from our lives slowly over time? Why is its value not encouraged more by employers?

Training and time are dedicated to the basics and repeatable tasks in an effort to gain efficiencies. But the gains we get are minimal and incremental at best. There is a better return on investment in creative automation and those ideas come from the creative types. Business leaders love to quote Henry Ford, "If I had asked people what they wanted, they would have said faster horses". Henry Ford was an inventor, a creator, a Rockstar.

Rock stars are artists. Passion comes with craft building. Being creative does not mean we are good at painting or drawing, it can mean a million different things to all different people. In the workforce, it can be creating beautiful PowerPoint presentations, writing elegant code, creating intuitive dashboards or even simply finding new ways to be organized and efficient in what you do. We all have the ability to be creative, but how good we are in our craft is dependent on how we flex our creative muscles. Those muscles can be worked on outside of the office in many different ways. Cooking a fancy meal, journaling, building crafts, working on puzzles are just a few ways we can expose ourselves to working on our right side of the brain.

If we want to excel in the workforce, we need to begin to take steps to take our crayons back. After self-experimentation over the last few months and learning to draw and paint after hours, I have experienced the following benefits outside while deep in creating:

1) Increased focus and flow in other parts of my life
2) Epiphanies on work and personal issues
3) Stress relief and a new type of active meditation
4) Increased confidence and pride of ownership
5) Realizations of being ok with mistakes, errors, and failures while having the ability to learn, correct and succeed in later iterations
6) Growing slowly as an artist and a professional

Don't just take my word for it. Grab a pen or pencil, a sheet of paper, some spices or even a needle and some yarn. Whatever interests you, begin experimenting with your creative side and flexing your creative muscles routinely and see if it does not help you in all other parts of your life.

"Life isn't about finding yourself. Life is about creating yourself."

-    Unknown

Embracing Boredom

One of the hardest activities we can partake in is just being and doing nothing, sitting in a daydream or staring at the clouds. This used to come easily to us as children but as we got older, we found less and less time for the activity of truly doing nothing. Our "nothing" time was replaced by "nothing" activities such as watching television or scrolling through our phones. Our anxiety spikes by the thought of being bored or doing nothing. We are consumed by the feeling of needing to be doing something, anything to make use of our time and fill it with value. The concept of time = money, where money = value, is beaten into us as we age. We then create a world for ourselves where we are unable to not fill every second of our waking time, for the most part, with non-valuable items. Similar to how a taxed muscle must be allowed to rest and recover, our brains must be allowed the same rest from time to time. Learn to be bored, the same way a child with nothing to do would.

A part of being bored is reigning in the part of the brain that is constantly seeking stimulation through our devices or other vices. Being bored allows us to be more creative. As the bored brain seeks stimulation from the ways it is addicted to and is denied those items, it begins to create thoughts and worlds inside your head. It unleashes its own anecdote to the need for simulation by spiking your creativity and letting you explore the world around you or inside your head. The difficult part is keeping negative thoughts out or rumination about the past or future. If you find yourself gravitating to a negative place, bring your focus back to the present with some deep breaths and focus on items or sounds around you.

Tip – Use the breathing technique portion of the Mindful Manager app to center yourself and bring your brain to a state of calm. After a few breaths, just take some time to sit, stare and observe the world around you.

Android
IOS

The Mindful Manager App (Just Breath)

Posture

When we were young, our parents and teachers told us to sit and stand up straight. As the digital age took over, we became consumed with our devices and digital lifestyle pulling our shoulders forward and arching our necks. Poor posture can cause a series of issues over time. Our bodies are designed for good posture, keeping our bones, organs and spine lined up without additional pressure. Bad posture leads to soreness and pain as it puts stress on our backs and constricts the lungs, making breathing slightly more difficult and decreasing blood circulation in the body.

As the muscles in our chest and abdominals weaken, we have a harder time enforcing corrective actions and the problems worsen. In addition to the strain and burden put on your lungs, the digestive tract is also disrupted as it bunches together. With a decrease in efficiency in the digestive tract, we open ourselves up to the risk of constipation and metabolic issues.

Bad posture from an aesthetic perspective is simply not an attractive one. Notice how you perceive others who are slouched over with shoulders rolled forward vs. those standing tall and straight? The latter are perceived to be more upbeat, full of energy and confidence. Body language plays a large part in how we feel and how we are perceived by others. Bad posture gives on the image of a lack of confidence, negativity, and general unpleasantness. The good news is that bad posture, over time, can be corrected. Let's discuss how we can correct it and why we would want to.

Since most of our lives require us to be seated, we must be sure we are sitting correctly. Most offices provide an ergonomic chair but it is simple to lose the help of the chair by sitting forward and not taking advantage of the contouring and lumbar support it is meant to provide. Sitting in good posture can be achieved in any reasonable chair. Sit with your back straight and shoulders back with your buttock pushed to the back of the chair. The height of the chair should be so that your knees are bent at ninety-degrees and your feet flat on the floor. Your arms, as they type, should be approximately at a ninety-degree angle at the elbows. The head should be looking straight ahead at the screen. If you need to give your screen or laptop a boost, a few books under the laptop should do the trick in a pinch if a stand is not available.

Standing desks have gained popularity over the last few years. Desks which can adjust easily from a seated position to standing. These desks can help play a great role in correcting posture problems by strengthening the legs, core, and back by keeping you in a standing position for longer periods of time. Just be sure the arms and neck stay at the same degree as if they were sitting so that they are not stretching awkwardly or forcing you to crane your neck to see the screen. Standing for long periods of time can put stress on the feet and knees. Soft foam mats are available and can alleviate some of this pain, but it is best to know when to take a rest and transition back to sitting to give the body a bit of rest.

Stretching and exercise play a large part in correcting your posture. Making sure your core is getting the strength training it requires in addition to the stretching and flexibility training obtained from activities like Yoga help keep the body aligned in the proper form.

In Eastern religions, there is the concept of Chakras. The Sanskrit word Chakra literally translates to wheel or disk. The term is used in Yoga practices and the chakras are visualized as seven wheels of energy in the body, starting from the base of the spine and reaching to the top of the head. It is believed each chakra connects the body to psychological, emotional, and spiritual states of being with the goal to keep each chakra open and flowing so that energy passes up, down and throughout the body to achieve a harmonious state of being. In my research, I found the practice of keeping the charkas aligned was not only a mental and spiritual exercise, but it also required a physical alignment of the spine, usually demonstrated through proper posture techniques for sitting and standing. Entire books have been dedicated to translate and explain the concept of chakras and energy, so I will not spend too much time digging into the details. If these principals and concepts intrigue you, I highly recommend doing your own research and coming to your own conclusions on the philosophies of chakras and spirituality. Below is a quick guide to the seven chakras of the body, and a diagram of how they fit in with the body and clean posture:

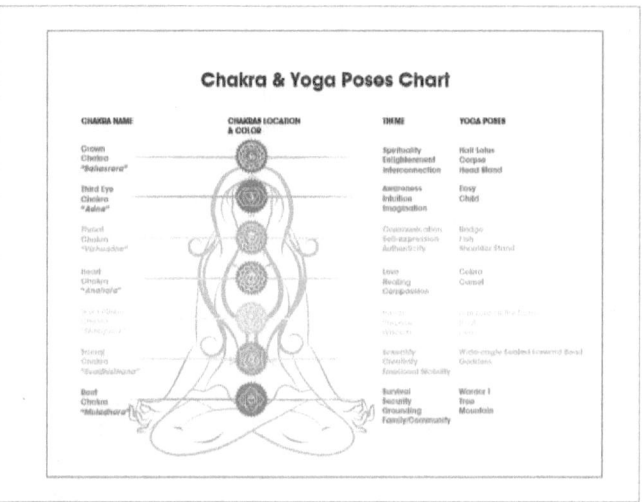

1. Root Chakra — Represents our foundation and feeling of being grounded.
Location: Base of spine in tailbone area.
Emotional issues: Survival issues such as financial independence, money, and food.

2. Sacral Chakra — Our connection and ability to accept others and new experiences.
Location: Lower abdomen, about two inches below the navel and two inches in.
Emotional issues: Sense of abundance, well-being, pleasure, and sexuality.

3. Solar Plexus Chakra — Our ability to be confident and in control of our lives.

Location: Upper abdomen in the stomach area.
Emotional issues: Self-worth, self-confidence, and self-esteem.

4. Heart Chakra — Our ability to love.
Location: Center of the chest just above the heart.
Emotional issues: Love, joy and inner peace.

5. Throat Chakra — Our ability to communicate.
Location: Throat.
Emotional issues: Communication, self-expression of feelings and the truth.

6. Third Eye Chakra — Our ability to focus on and see the big picture.
Location: Forehead between the eyes (also called the Brow Chakra).
Emotional issues: Intuition, imagination, wisdom and the ability to think and make decisions.

7. Crown Chakra — The highest chakra represents our ability to be fully connected spiritually.
Location: The very top of the head.
Emotional issues: Inner and outer beauty, our connection to spirituality and pure bliss.

Inbox Zero, Declutter your email

The concept of Inbox Zero is a simple one and connects back to the concepts of decluttering, cleaning, minimalism and killing the notifications. Inbox Zero was developed by productivity expert, Merlin Mann. According to Mann, the zero is not a reference to the number of messages in an inbox; it is "the amount of time an employee's brain is in his inbox." Mann's point is that time and attention are finite and when an inbox is confused with a "to-do" list, productivity suffers.

I have witnessed the screens of fellow coworkers with over thirty-thousand unread messages or emails. This digital space consumes mental space in the brain. It signals uncompleted items, tasks, and data that need to be processed and possibly actioned on. Letting your inbox become untidy does not lead to engaging productive work. Set up a practice of reaching Inbox Zero, where all items have been either read, removed or moved to a longer-term to-do list or your micro to-do list where they are much more likely to reach a state of action and completion.

Cut Yourself Some Slack

Productivity and creative energy are finite. Once you have expended what is in the reserves, it will be imperative that a break is taken or there will be diminishing returns. We all deserve a break from time to time to refill the tank and get some much-deserved rest. This should not create a feeling of guilt but rather an appreciation of self-love and giving yourself the time needed to rest and be content with the work put in thus far.

Add a cheat period into your week from time to time. Maybe it is a meal where you do not obsess about the calorie count or an evening where you purposely do not work on any other projects and just watch television. Allowing a cheat into the schedule will give you something to look forward to and give the brain a shot of that feel-good chemical it needs to help curb cravings during the other parts of the week. Going cold turkey and making hard life changes at once usually fail, as this creates a shock to the brain and body. There is a pendulum effect as the habits and routines take hold and fall to the wayside, usually driven more by guilt and feelings of failure rather than a true feeling of improvement and self-worth.

Use weekends as rest periods. Sleep in a bit later or stay up a bit longer. Do that one thing you love that is not related to personal growth or gain. Spend time with family and friends. Even if you are an introvert, there are psychological benefits to being around others even for a short period of time. It is human nature to be in a pack and be part of a community. It is how our early ancestors were able to survive harsh conditions and carry forward. Find quality people to spend some quality time with for however long you are comfortable.

"As long as you're learning, you're not failing"

- Bob Ross

Conclusion. Small Changes and Small Shifts

This book was created by using a lot of the practices and methods mentioned in this book. It was the only way to complete it and hit my writing goals in addition to having a fast-paced and demanding job, personal life commitments and being sure to take the appropriate time for rest, family and friends. There is a lot to digest and to put into practice, but over the last few years, and even now, I only consistently abide by 60-80% of the practices at a time. Doing them all is quite a difficult task. Each skill takes time, practice, focus, and commitment to master and those are hard items for even the most seasoned practitioners of Mindful Manager's techniques. The goal should be to make small changes and small shifts at a pace you are comfortable with. Do not think about changing all at once and in one shot. That would be gearing yourself up for failure. Think of your future self, four or five years out. Think of how different that person will be even with just one small shift daily. That person will be unrecognizable from who they are today. If you are able to get out of your own head and see the bigger picture, make a promise to your future self that you will not procrastinate on a single small change today and get to work. Visualize how grateful that person will be and use that as your motivation to get to work!

There is no secret sauce or lifehack that is waiting to be discovered that will lead you to happiness and success. It all comes down to hard work, motivation, focus, and passion at the end of the day, while fighting off the distractions of the modern world. I hope you get some value out of this book and start managing your life mindfully. And remember, just take a second to stop, slow down and breath when you need it.

Books Recommendations

1) Deep Work – Cal Newport
2) Rework - David Heinemeier Hansson and Jason Fried
3) Storms can't Hurt the Sky - Gabriel Cohen
4) The subtle art of not giving a f*** - Mark Manson
5) Steal Like an Artist: 10 Things Nobody Told You About Being Creative - Austin Kleon
6) Declutter your Mind - Barrie Davenport and S. J. Scott
7) 10% Happier – Dan Harris

My Other Books

4) Jack of All Trades Master of Some; An Introduction to Consulting
5) An Introduction to Consulting - A Primer: An abridged and essentials guide from the book: Jack of All Trades Master of Some, an Introduction to Consulting
6) The Solar System; A STEM book for children

www.ingramcontent.com/pod-product-compliance
Lightning Source LLC
Chambersburg PA
CBHW020924180526
45163CB00007B/2874